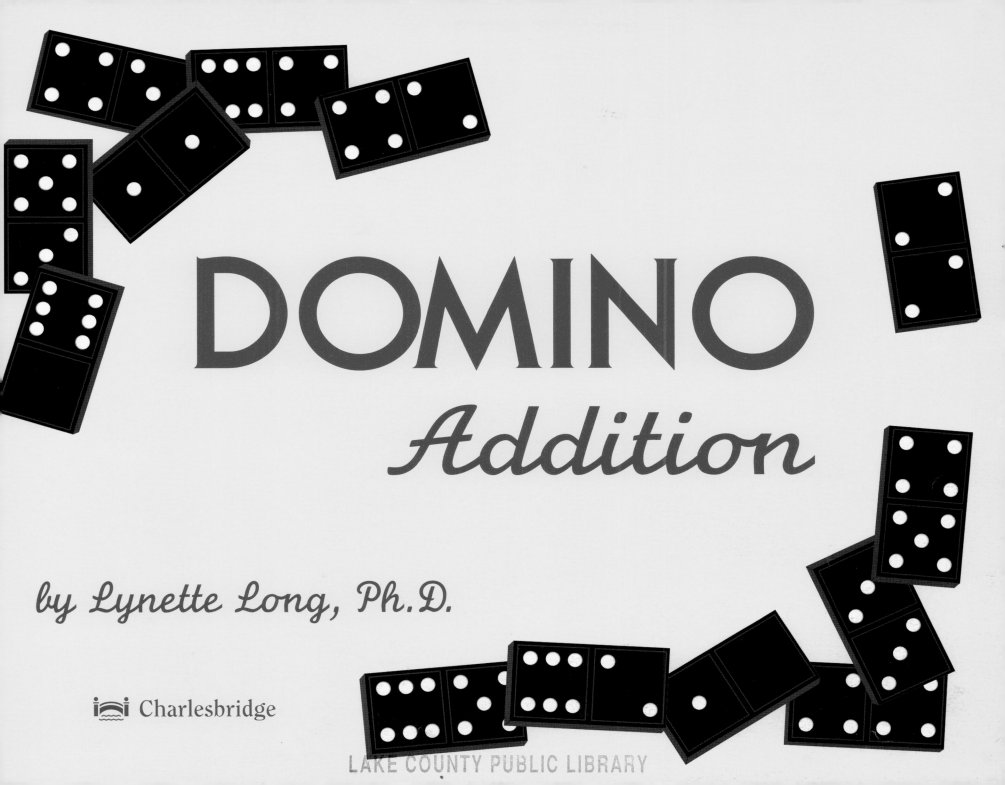

DOMINO
Addition

by Lynette Long, Ph.D.

Charlesbridge

To my dad, whose constant
creativity is an inspiration to me.
— L.L.

Published by Charlesbridge Publishing
85 Main Street
Watertown, MA 02172-4411
(617) 926-0329

Printed in Hong Kong
(sc) 10 9 8 7 6 5 4 3 2
(hc) 10 9 8 7 6 5 4 3 2

Library of Congress Cataloging-in-Publication Data
Long, Lynette.
Domino addition / by Lynette Long. — 1st ed.
p.   cm.
Summary: Explains basic addition through the use
of dominoes.
ISBN 0-88106-878-0 (hardcover)
ISBN 0-88106-879-9 (library reinforced)
ISBN 0-88106-877-2 (softcover)
1. Addition — Juvenile literature. 2. Dominoes —
Juvenile literature. [1. Addition. 2. Dominoes.] I. Title.
QA115.L72 1996
513.2'11 — dc20   95-20083
                                          CIP
                                          AC

The illustrations in this book are done in Adobe Illustrator.
The display type and text type were set in ITC Benguiat Gothic,
Serif Gothic, and Monoline Script.
Color separations were made by The Arthur Morgan Publishing Co.
Printed and bound by Elegance Printing & Binding Co. Ltd.
Production supervision by Brian G. Walker
Designed by Diane M. Earley

This book is like a treasure hunt! You can
search each picture for the dominoes
with the right number of spots. And
when you are done, you can check your
work. Turn the page and find the answer
in the corner. But remember, pick the
dominoes on your own first. No peeking!

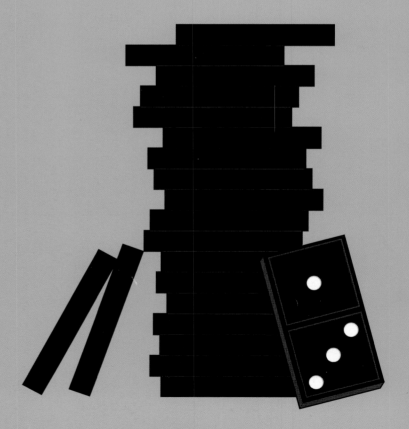

Learning to add is fun, especially when you use dominoes. It's easy! Let's learn how.

Dominoes have two halves. Each half may have zero, one, two, three, four, five, or six spots.

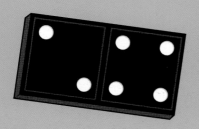 A domino can have three spots on one half and zero spots on the other half, or

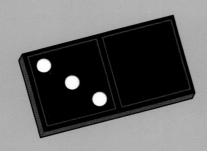 two spots on one half and four spots on the other half, or even

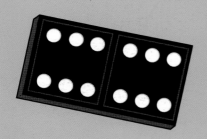 six spots on one half and six spots on the other half!

Here is a complete set of dominoes.

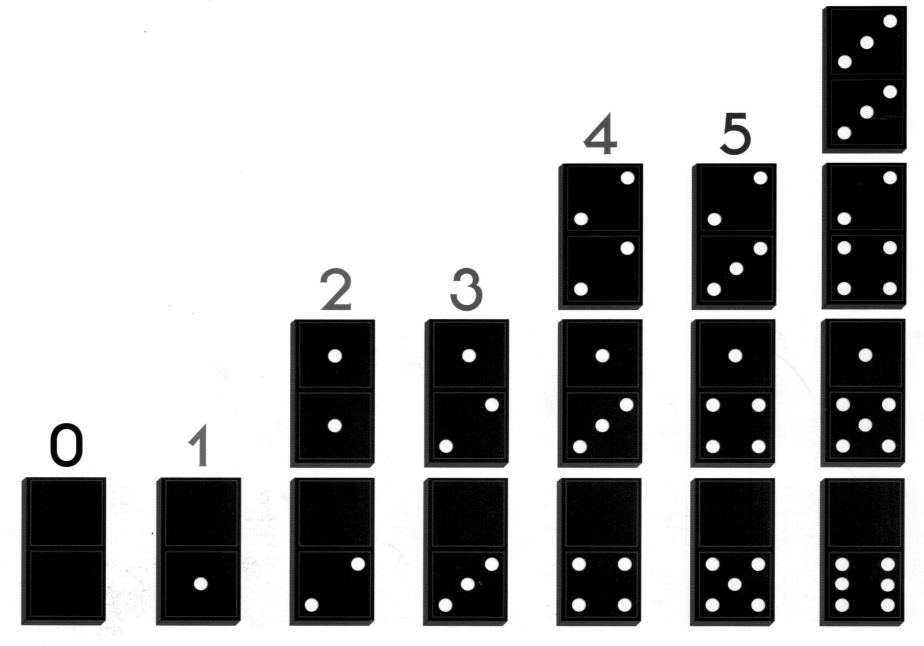

You can **add** the spots to find the total number of spots on each domino.

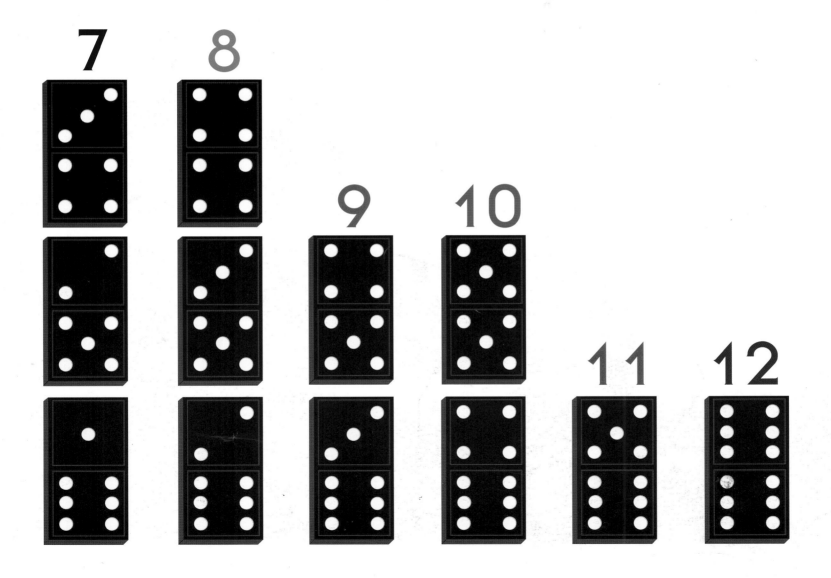

Add the number of spots on the top half of this domino to the number of spots on the bottom half.

$$
\begin{array}{r}
0 \\
+\,0 \\
\hline
0
\end{array}
$$

The total is **ZERO**!

Can you find the domino that has a total of **ZERO** spots?

Add the number of spots on the top half of this domino to the number of spots on the bottom half.

$$1$$
$$+0$$
$$\overline{}$$
$$1$$

The total is **ONE**!

Point to the domino that has a total of **ONE** spot.

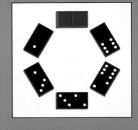

Add the number of spots on the top half of each domino to the number of spots on the bottom half of each domino.

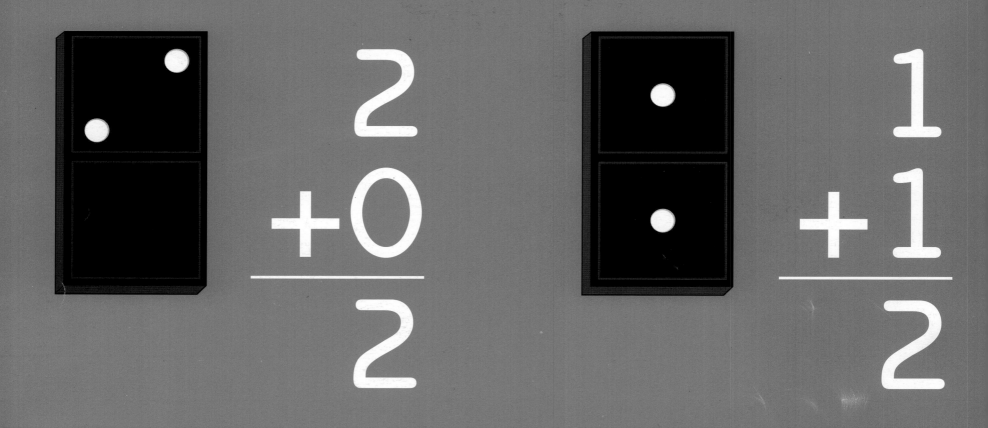

$$\begin{array}{r} 2 \\ +0 \\ \hline 2 \end{array}$$

$$\begin{array}{r} 1 \\ +1 \\ \hline 2 \end{array}$$

The total is **TWO**!

Where are the dominoes that have a total of **TWO** spots?

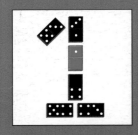

Add the number of spots on the top half of each domino to the number of spots on the bottom half of each domino.

$$\begin{array}{r} 3 \\ +0 \\ \hline 3 \end{array}$$

$$\begin{array}{r} 2 \\ +1 \\ \hline 3 \end{array}$$

The total is **THREE**!

Find the dominoes that have a total of **THREE** spots.

Add the number of spots on the top half of each domino to the number of spots on the bottom half of each domino.

$$\begin{array}{r} 4 \\ +0 \\ \hline 4 \end{array}$$

$$\begin{array}{r} 3 \\ +1 \\ \hline 4 \end{array}$$

$$\begin{array}{r} 2 \\ +2 \\ \hline 4 \end{array}$$

The total is **FOUR!**

Which dominoes have
a total of **FOUR** spots?

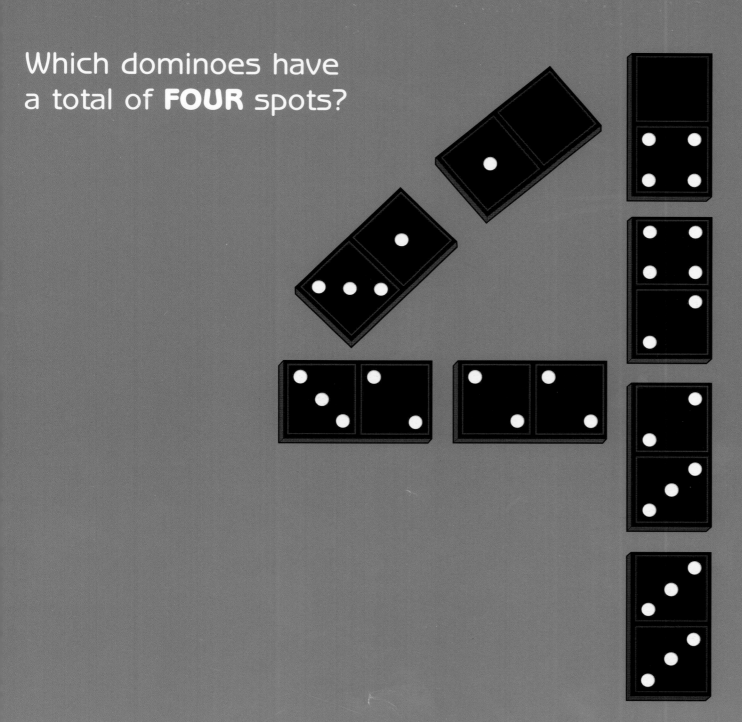

Add the number of spots on the top half of each domino to the number of spots on the bottom half of each domino.

$$\begin{array}{r} 5 \\ +0 \\ \hline 5 \end{array}$$

$$\begin{array}{r} 4 \\ +1 \\ \hline 5 \end{array}$$

$$\begin{array}{r} 3 \\ +2 \\ \hline 5 \end{array}$$

The total is **FIVE**!

Search for the
dominoes that have
a total of **FIVE** spots.

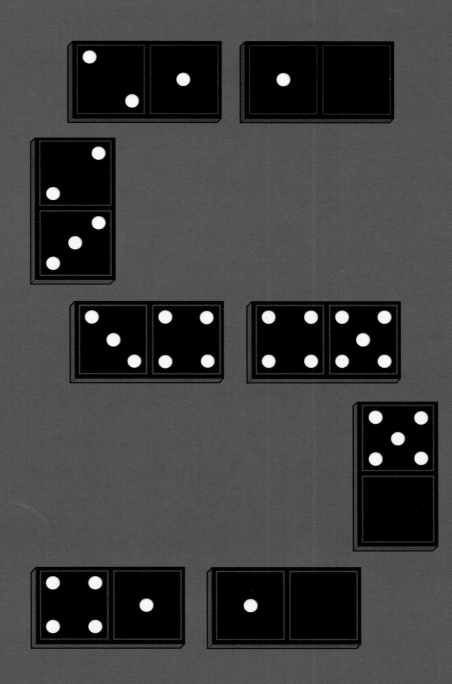

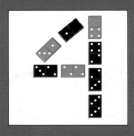

Add the number of spots on the top half of each domino to the number of spots on the bottom half of each domino.

$$\begin{array}{r} 6 \\ +0 \\ \hline 6 \end{array}$$

$$\begin{array}{r} 5 \\ +1 \\ \hline 6 \end{array}$$

$$\begin{array}{r} 4 \\ +2 \\ \hline 6 \end{array}$$

$$\begin{array}{r} 3 \\ +3 \\ \hline 6 \end{array}$$

The total is **SIX**!

Can you find the dominoes that have a total of **SIX** spots?

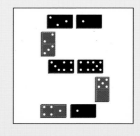

Add the number of spots on the top half of each domino to the number of spots on the bottom half of each domino.

$$\begin{array}{r} 6 \\ +1 \\ \hline 7 \end{array}$$

$$\begin{array}{r} 5 \\ +2 \\ \hline 7 \end{array}$$

$$\begin{array}{r} 4 \\ +3 \\ \hline 7 \end{array}$$

The total is **SEVEN**!

Point to the dominoes that have a total of **SEVEN** spots.

Add the number of spots on the top half of each domino to the number of spots on the bottom half of each domino.

$$\begin{array}{r} 6 \\ +2 \\ \hline 8 \end{array}$$

$$\begin{array}{r} 5 \\ +3 \\ \hline 8 \end{array}$$

$$\begin{array}{r} 4 \\ +4 \\ \hline 8 \end{array}$$

The total is **EIGHT**!

Where are the dominoes that have a total of **EIGHT** spots?

Add the number of spots on the top half of each domino to the number of spots on the bottom half of each domino.

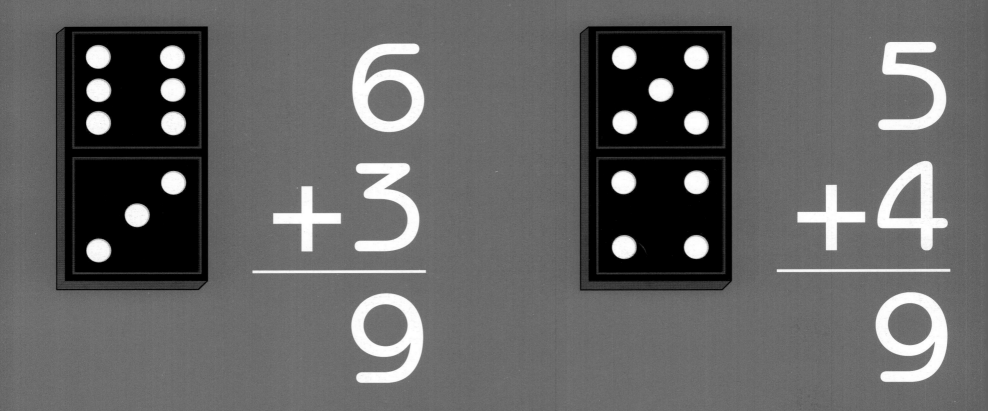

$$\begin{array}{r} 6 \\ +3 \\ \hline 9 \end{array}$$

$$\begin{array}{r} 5 \\ +4 \\ \hline 9 \end{array}$$

The total is **NINE!**

Find the dominoes that have a total of **NINE** spots.

Add the number of spots on the top half of each domino to the number of spots on the bottom half of each domino.

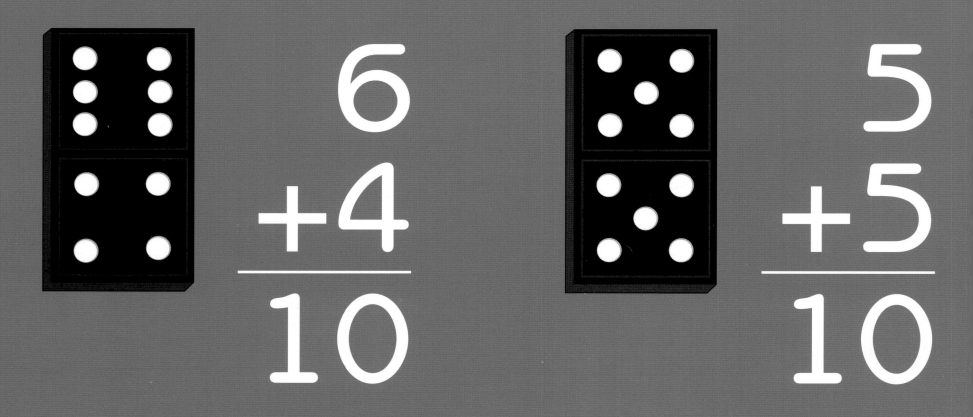

$$\begin{array}{r} 6 \\ +4 \\ \hline 10 \end{array}$$

$$\begin{array}{r} 5 \\ +5 \\ \hline 10 \end{array}$$

The total is **TEN!**

Which dominoes have a total of **TEN** spots?

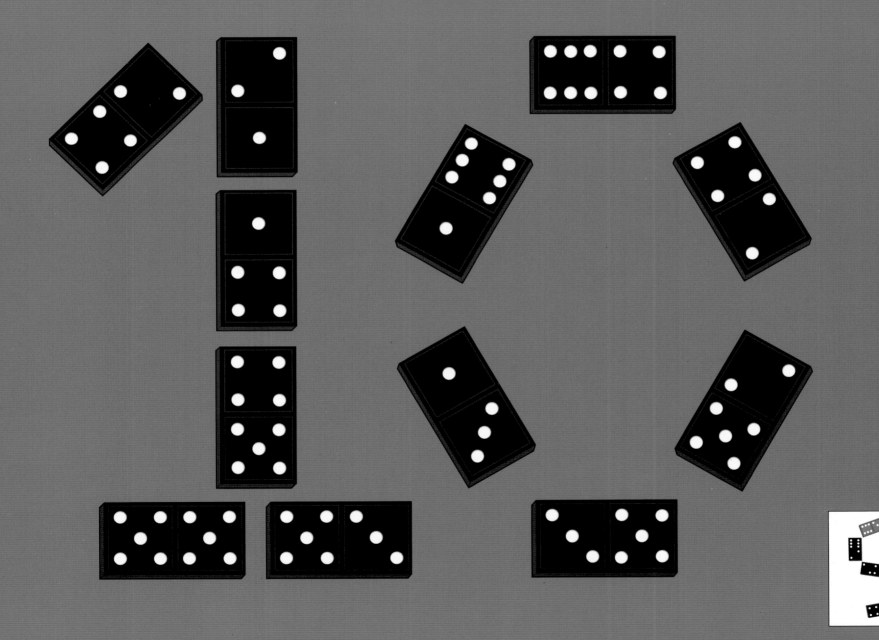

Add the number of spots on the top half of this domino to the number of spots on the bottom half.

6
+5
___
11

The total is **ELEVEN**!

Search for the domino that has a total of **ELEVEN** spots.

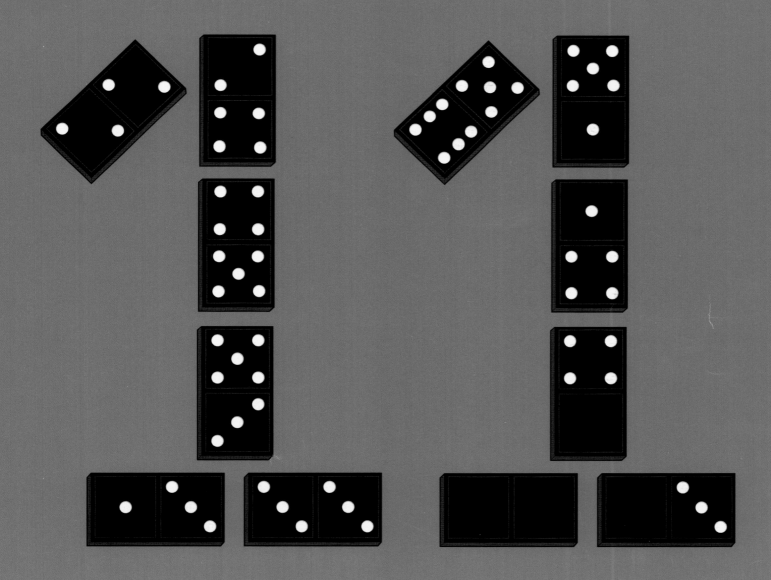

Add the number of spots on the top half of this domino to the number of spots on the bottom half.

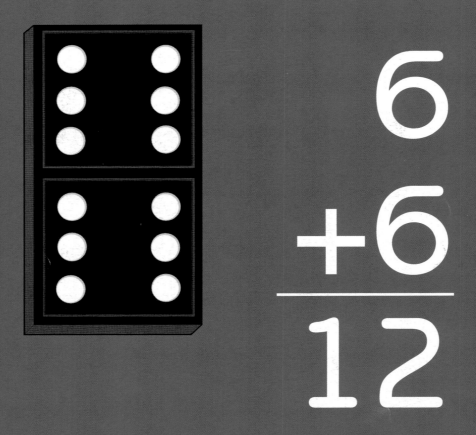

6
+6
―――
12

The total is **TWELVE!**

Can you find the domino that has a total of **TWELVE** spots?

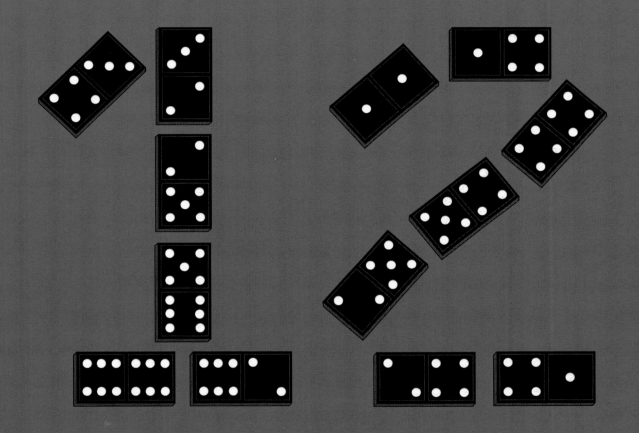

Congratulations! You have learned how to add up to **TWELVE**! Did you have fun?

Now, turn the page to see what you have done.

0 + 0 = **0**

1 + 0 = **1**

2 + 0 =
1 + 1 = **2**

3 + 0 =
2 + 1 = **3**

4 + 0 =
3 + 1 =
2 + 2 = **4**

5 + 0 =
4 + 1 =
3 + 2 = **5**

6 + 0 =
5 + 1 =
4 + 2 =
3 + 3 = **6**

6 + 1 =
5 + 2 =
4 + 3 = **7**

6 + 2 =
5 + 3 =
4 + 4 = **8**

6 + 3 =
5 + 4 = **9**

6 + 4 =
5 + 5 = **10**

6 + 5 = **11**

6 + 6 = **12**

0 1 2 3 4 5 6 7 8 9 10 11 12